Tornadoes

Written by

Contents

Tornadoes 2
People in Danger 4
Keeping Safe 8
Wildlife in Danger 10
Studying Tornadoes.......... 14
Index........................ 17

Tornadoes

Tornadoes happen almost everywhere in the world. They can happen at any time of the day.

They start when warm air and cold air mix. The air makes a funnel. The funnel comes down from a thundercloud. It spins very, very fast and it can suck things up from the ground and into the air.

The wind inside a tornado can be very strong and fast.

Tornadoes are very dangerous and can do a lot of damage to people and houses. They can also do a lot of damage to the land and animals.

thundercloud

direction of the wind

funnel of spinning air

tornado

The tornado forms in a thundercloud.

People in Danger

When a tornado comes, people are in danger. Many people can be killed or hurt.

A tornado can destroy a town. It can blow roofs off houses and lift buildings. It can lift cars and even trains up into the air! Sometimes whole houses can be sucked up.

Heavy things that are picked up by a tornado are very dangerous. They can fly through the air fast and hurt or kill people.

A tornado destroyed this town. It left thousands of people with no homes.

A tornado can rip a house into pieces.

About 1000 tornadoes hit the United States of America every year. There is a place there that is called Tornado Alley. More tornadoes happen in Tornado Alley than anywhere else in the world.

Tornado Alley is found in the United States of America.

North America

Tornado Alley

Close-up of part of North America

Keeping Safe

People who live where there are tornadoes have ways to keep safe.

During a storm, people can listen to weather reports to see if a tornado has been seen. They can watch for signs that a tornado is going to happen. Signs can be:

- the sky sometimes turns a greenish black
- there are big thunderstorm clouds
- there may be a loud sound like a waterfall or a train
- there are strong winds
- there is heavy rain
- there is hail.

Some people have special shelters in their backyards. These are built underground. They have heavy doors that can be tightly closed. If there are signs of a tornado coming, people can go to their shelter.

The shelter can have:

- a radio with a battery

- a torch

- a first-aid kit

- blankets

- water

- food

- clothes

- any medicines they need.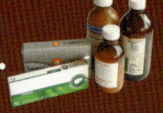

Wildlife in Danger

Animals can be killed or hurt by a tornado, too.

Tornadoes can also destroy the land and forests where animals live. They can break the branches and pull the leaves and bark off trees. Sometimes they lift the trees right out of the ground.

When a forest is destroyed by a tornado, many animals die. Those animals that survive are left with no homes. It takes many years for a forest to grow again.

Some animals know when a tornado is going to happen. This can sometimes give them time to find a safe place. Some insects hide in cracks. Fish swim to deeper parts of streams and lakes. Birds will fly away or hide in trees, and many seabirds stay on the shore.

Horses know when a tornado is coming, too. They gallop fast around their paddock. They can be one of the best warning signs of a tornado coming!

Studying Tornadoes

Some scientists study tornadoes. They try to find out when they are going to happen.

They look for big thunderclouds that could become a tornado. They use a radar. The radar can tell scientists if a storm is coming closer or moving away. The scientists can then warn people before a tornado starts.

Scientists can measure a tornado. They can measure the speed of the wind. They can then know the kind of damage a tornado can do.

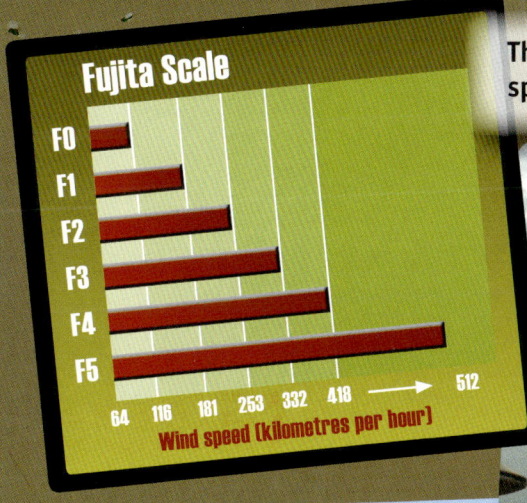

The Fujita Scale can measure the speed of the wind in a tornado.

A radar can be used on a truck and on land.

Some people like to chase tornadoes and study them. These people are called stormchasers. They look for weather that is just right for a big thunderstorm. They find the place where the storm is and wait for tornadoes to happen. They can tell which way a tornado is moving and they know how to keep out of its way. When they get near a tornado, they have only a few minutes to use their gear. Then they have to get out of the way quickly!

But the information they get could help keep people safe.

Most people move away from a tornado, but stormchasers drive towards it!

Index

damage by tornadoes
    to animals 2, 10
    to people 2, 4, 7

keeping safe from tornadoes
    animals 12
    people 8-9

places where tornaodes happen
    . . . . 2, 6

stormchasers 16

studying tornadoes
    radar 14
    warning signs 8, 12
    wind speed 15

17

Reports

Tornadoes is a report.

A report has a topic:

> **Tornadoes**

A report has headings:

> **People in Danger**

> **Studying Tornadoes**

> **Keeping Safe**

> **Wildlife in Danger**

Some information is put under headings.

> **Keeping Safe**
>
> During a storm, people can listen to weather reports to see if a tornado is coming.
>
> Some people have special shelters in their backyards.

Information can be shown in other ways. This report has . . .

Labels

Map

Captions

Photographs

Diagrams

Graph

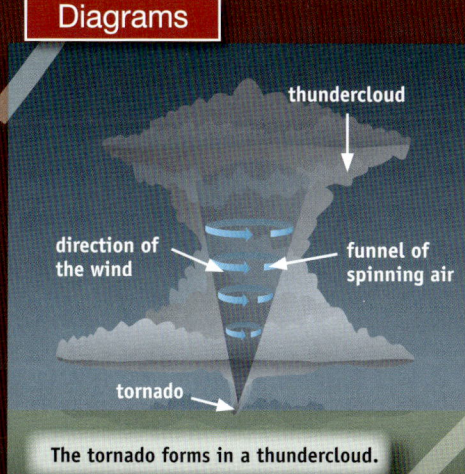

The tornado forms in a thundercloud.

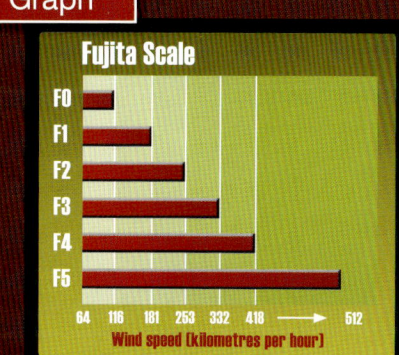

19

Guide Notes

Title: Tornadoes
Stage: Fluency

Text Form: Informational Report
Approach: Guided Reading
Processes: Thinking Critically, Exploring Language, Processing Information
Written and Visual Focus: Contents Page, Illustrative Diagram, Captions, Labels, Maps, Bullet Points, Index

THINKING CRITICALLY
(sample questions)

Before Reading – Establishing Prior Knowledge
- What do you know about tornadoes?

Visualising the Text Content
- What might you expect to see in this book?
- What form of writing do you think will be used by the author?

Look at the contents page and index. Encourage the students to think about the information and make predictions about the text content.

After Reading – Interpreting the Text
- What do you think the weather could be like before a tornado forms?
- Do you think the material a house is built from would make any difference when a tornado comes? Why do you think that?
- Which of the items kept in the shelter would be the most important to have? Why do you think that?
- What do you think might help an animal survive in a tornado?
- How do you think animals know when a tornado is going to happen?
- How much damage do you think a small tornado on the Fujita Scale would cause, compared to a large tornado on the Fujita Scale?
- What do you know about tornadoes that you didn't know before?
- What things in the book helped you to understand the information?
- What questions do you have after reading the text?

EXPLORING LANGUAGE

Terminology
Photograph credits, index, contents page, imprint information, ISBN number